ARCTIC LAND MAMMALS

Published by Inhabit Media Inc.
www.inhabitmedia.com

Inhabit Media Inc. (Iqaluit) 2434 Paurngaq Cres., Iqaluit, Nunavut, X0A 2H0
(Toronto) 612 Mount Pleasant Rd., Toronto, ON, M4S 2M8

Design and layout copyright © 2025 by Inhabit Media Inc.
Text copyright © 2025 by Brian Koonoo (Arctic Fox); William Flaherty (Arctic Wolf and Polar Bear); Allen Niptanatiak (Muskox and Wolverine); Dorothy and David Aglukark (Caribou); Monica Ittusardjuat (Lemming and Arctic Hare); Jaypeetee Arnakak (Inuit Qaujimajatuqangit).
Illustrations by Joseph Starkey (Arctic Fox); Sean Bigham (Arctic Wolf); Kagan McLeod (Muskox); Amiel Sandland (Caribou); Danny Christopher (Polar Bear); Patricia Ann Lewis-MacDougall (Wolverine); Lenny Lishchenko (Arctic Hare and Lemming) copyright © 2025 Inhabit Media Inc.

Editors: Neil Christopher and Anne Fullerton
Art Directors: Danny Christopher and Astrid Arijanto
Designer: Fabiana Marino and Drew Gravelle

All rights reserved. The use of any part of this publication reproduced, transmitted in any form or by any means, electronic, mechanical, photocopying, recording, or otherwise, or stored in a retrievable system, without written consent of the publisher, is an infringement of copyright law.

We acknowledge the support of the Canada Council for the Arts for our publishing program.

This project was made possible in part by the Government of Canada.

ISBN: 978-1-77227-585-8

Printed in Canada

TABLE OF CONTENTS

2	ALL ABOUT ARCTIC LAND MAMMALS
4	What Is a Mammal?
6	Predators and Prey
8	Arctic Adaptations
10	Inuit Qaujimajatuqangit
12	Traditional Uses
14	ARCTIC LAND MAMMALS UP CLOSE
16	Arctic Fox
20	Arctic Hare
24	Arctic Wolf
28	Caribou
32	Lemming
36	Muskox
40	Polar Bear
44	Wolverine
48	AUTHORS
49	GLOSSARY OF INUKTITUT WORDS

ALL ABOUT ARCTIC LAND MAMMALS

What Is a Mammal?

Mammals are **vertebrates**, which means they have a backbone. They breathe air and grow hair. Female mammals make milk for their babies. Mammals tend to have a more complex brain than other animals.

Mammals can live in almost any habitat—on or under the ground, in trees, and even in water. Arctic land mammals are ones that live on the ground, and who live in the Arctic. Because mammals can control their own body temperature, they can survive in different climates.

Lemming

Polar Bear

Arctic land mammals can be as small as a lemming or an Arctic hare, and as large as a polar bear or a muskox!

Most mammals are protective of their young. They feed them, protect them from predators, and teach them how to survive.

Humans are mammals!

Predators and Prey

Every animal eats other living things to survive. These living things can be plants, animals, or both. **Predators** hunt other animals, and **prey** are the animals that are hunted. Arctic wolves and polar bears are **apex predators**, which means no other animal hunts them (except humans). Animals like Arctic foxes and wolverines are **scavengers**, which means they eat leftovers from other predators' hunts.

Prey animals like Arctic hares and caribou use their speed and strong senses of hearing and smell to avoid predators. Predators like Arctic wolves work together to feed their pack. Arctic wolves hunt large animals like muskoxen as a team.

Polar bears wait patiently for seals at breathing holes on the sea ice. The bears' great sense of smell and sharp claws and teeth make them excellent hunters. Polar bears can also swim up to seals that are resting on ice floes and catch them from below.

Muskoxen work together to protect themselves from Arctic wolves. The most powerful members of the muskox herd will stay on the outside of the herd, protecting the young and weak members on the inside. Muskoxen use their strength, size, and horns to keep predators away.

Arctic Adaptations

The Arctic is too cold for many species to survive. But Arctic land mammals adapt to make the North their home.

Escaping the Wind: Some Arctic mammals (like lemmings and Arctic foxes) dig and burrow underground to escape the cold wind. Others (like muskoxen and baby lemmings) will huddle together in a group to keep warm.

Fat: Some Arctic mammals (like muskoxen, caribou, and polar bears) have extra layers of fat that help keep them warm. It also helps them store energy for when their food supplies are low.

Camouflage: Some have white fur (like polar bears), or fur that turns white in the winter months (like Arctic foxes and Arctic hares). This allows them to hide in their snowy surroundings.

Compact: The longer an animal's features are, the longer it takes for them to warm up. That's why many Arctic mammals (like Arctic foxes, Arctic wolves, and caribou) have shorter ears and snouts than their southern relatives.

Fur: Many have thick fur to keep them warm. Some (like muskoxen and Arctic wolves) have 2 layers of fur to give them even more protection.

Fur Layers

Inuit Qaujimajatuqangit

Inuit Qaujimajatuqangit (IQ) are principles that come from a belief that humans and animals all have souls, and deserve respect and dignity.

For Inuit, treating animals and the land well is very important.

Arctic Fox Trap

Inuit only take what is needed when hunting, so that the animals will always be there.

Taking care of the land is important because it is the home of humans and animals. Inuit use an area of land for a time and then move to another area. This lets the animals, plants, and land recover.

It's important to value and protect our unique animals and the places where they live.

Traditional Uses

Inuit have been using animals for thousands of years.

Many mammals, like caribou and muskoxen, are hunted and eaten to provide energy and vitamins.

Mammal skin is used to make warm clothing. The fur of animals like muskoxen, Arctic foxes, Arctic hares, and wolverines is used to trim that clothing. The skin and fur of the muskox used to be used as bedding.

Muskox Wool

Muskox Stew

Tendons from mammals were used to make string and thread.

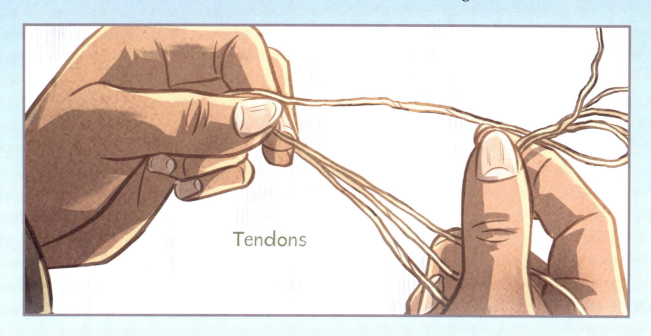

Tendons

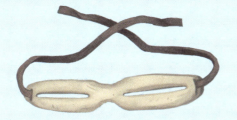

Snow Goggles

Ulu

The bones of some mammals, like caribou, were used to make tools and even snow goggles.

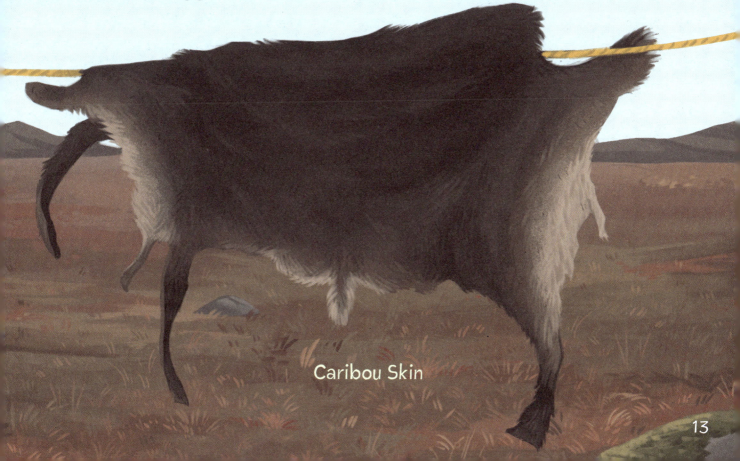

Caribou Skin

ARCTIC LAND MAMMALS UP CLOSE

Arctic Fox

The Arctic fox is found on the tundra and on the sea ice, depending on the season. During winter, they are found close to or on the sea ice.

Illustrated by: Joseph Starkey

Range

Arctic foxes live in all polar regions around the world, including the Canadian Arctic, Greenland, Iceland, and Arctic Europe. They are more plentiful in areas where there are lots of lemmings, which is their main food source. An Arctic fox has a home range that spans about 15 square miles (24 kilometres).

Babies

Arctic fox babies are called "kits," "pups," or "whelps." Babies are usually born in the spring inside dens close to the banks of lakes and rivers. Each litter has 11 to 16 babies. That is one of the largest litter sizes of any mammal in the world! The babies stay with their mother in the den for about 3.5 months. They drink only their mother's milk for about the first 5 or 6 weeks, and then they eat the meat that their parents bring them.

Diet

Arctic foxes eat lemmings, ringed seal pups, Arctic hares, birds, and eggs. They are predators, but they also scavenge. They often follow polar bears to eat the leftovers of their seal hunts. During times when food is scarce, Arctic foxes may even eat insects, animal droppings, or berries.

Lemming   Arctic Hare

Skeleton

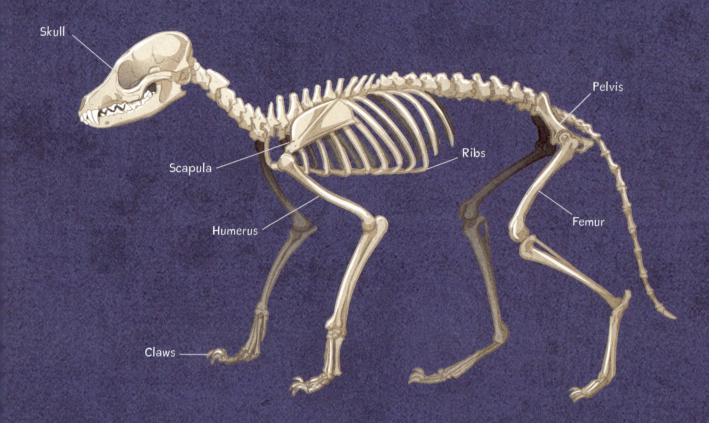

- Skull
- Scapula
- Humerus
- Claws
- Ribs
- Pelvis
- Femur

Ears and Nose

They use their keen senses to hear and smell lemmings hiding in the **subnivean space**—the space between the ground and the snow.

Claws and Paws

Their claws and paws are built for digging in dirt and snow, which helps them find prey.

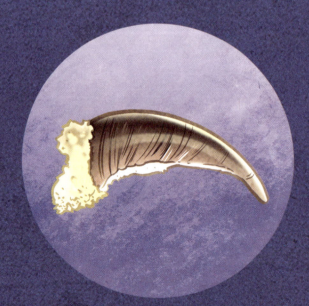

Arctic Fox Claw

Fun Facts

Arctic foxes will travel very long distances to find food. They are excellent swimmers and can swim between islands to find food or escape predators. An Arctic fox wearing a satellite collar once travelled nearly 2,175 miles (3,500 kilometres) from Norway to Canada! The trek took the fox 76 days, and 21 of those days were spent on the sea ice.

Map of Arctic Fox Trek from Norway to Ellesmere Island, Canada

Weight
7 to 17 pounds (3 to 8 kilograms)

Length
2.5 to 3.5 feet (76 to 107 centimetres)

Arctic Hare

Arctic hares can run very fast—up to 40 miles (64 kilometres) per hour! They can stand and even hop on their hind legs to get a better look at their surroundings. Arctic hares don't often swim, but they can in order to escape from predators. Some Arctic hares live alone, while others live in family groups. You can spot Arctic hares gathered together eating moss and twigs—sometimes in groups as big as 50!

Illustrated by: Lenny Lishchenko

Range

Arctic hares live farther north than any other hare. They live throughout the northern tundra regions of Canada and Greenland. They tend to stay close to their burrows in case they need to escape a predator.

Babies

Arctic hare babies are called "leverets." There are usually 2 to 8 leverets in a litter, and they are born in the spring or summer. The mother will build a nest in the ground, where it is protected by rocks or bush. The babies will stay close to their mother until they're about 9 weeks old.

Diet

Arctic willow makes up about 90 percent of an Arctic hare's diet. They also eat other woody plants, lichen, moss, leaves, roots, and berries. They have a great sense of sight and smell, which helps them find food under the snow. Arctic hares will sometimes go onto sea ice to find seaweed to eat!

Lichen   Cloudberries

Skeleton

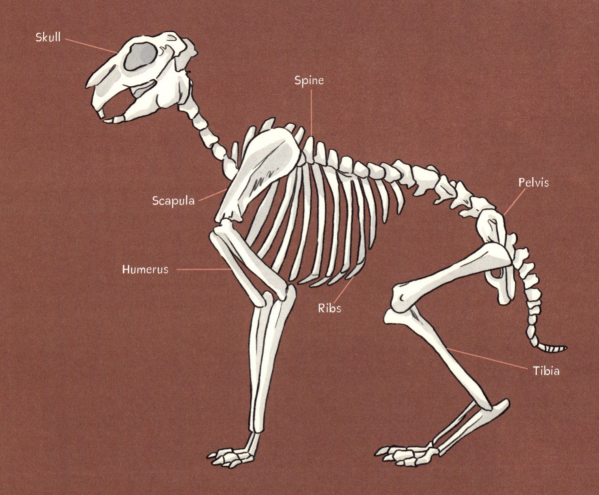

Claws

Their sharp claws help them dig through icy snow.

Teeth

Their front teeth are the longest of any hare, and help them pull plants from the ground.

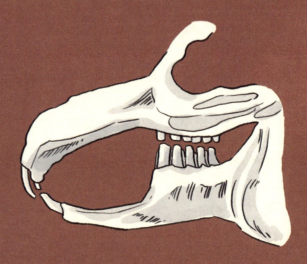

Fun Facts

Arctic hares' eyes are located on the sides of their heads, which allows them to see all around them without moving their necks. They have dark eyelashes that act like sunglasses, protecting them from the sun. They are **nocturnal**, which means they are awake during the night, but they have excellent vision and can see in the dark.

Weight
5 to 15 pounds (2 to 7 kilograms)

Length
20 to 27 inches (51 to 69 centimetres)

Arctic Wolf

Arctic wolves are lean and tall, but they have smaller ears and shorter noses than grey wolves. Sometimes Arctic wolves roam very far to find food, and they can travel great distances in a single day. Arctic wolves are fast, and can run up to 40 miles (about 64 kilometres) per hour.

Illustrated by: Sean Bigham

Range

Arctic wolves are found in Greenland and the Arctic regions of Canada and Alaska. They are mostly found on land, and sometimes on the sea ice.

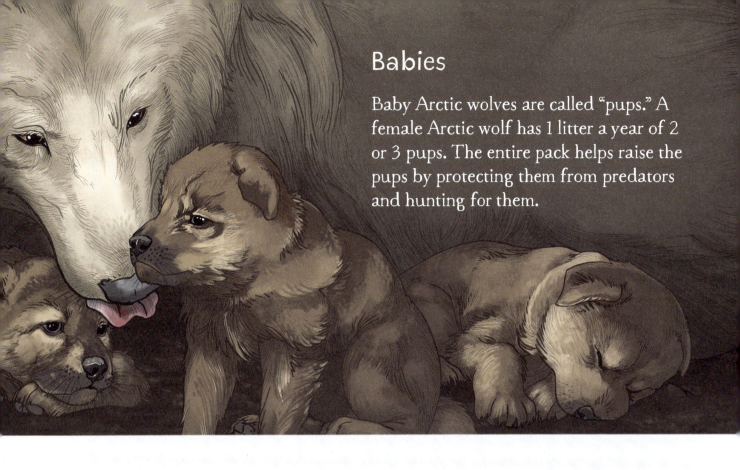

Babies

Baby Arctic wolves are called "pups." A female Arctic wolf has 1 litter a year of 2 or 3 pups. The entire pack helps raise the pups by protecting them from predators and hunting for them.

Diet

Arctic wolves hunt muskoxen, caribou, Arctic hares, and seal pups. They've also been seen eating lemmings, fish, birds, and bird eggs. Arctic wolves almost always hunt large prey in packs. An Arctic wolf can eat up to 20 pounds (about 9 kilograms) of meat at once!

Arctic Hare

Muskoxen

Seal Pup

Skeleton

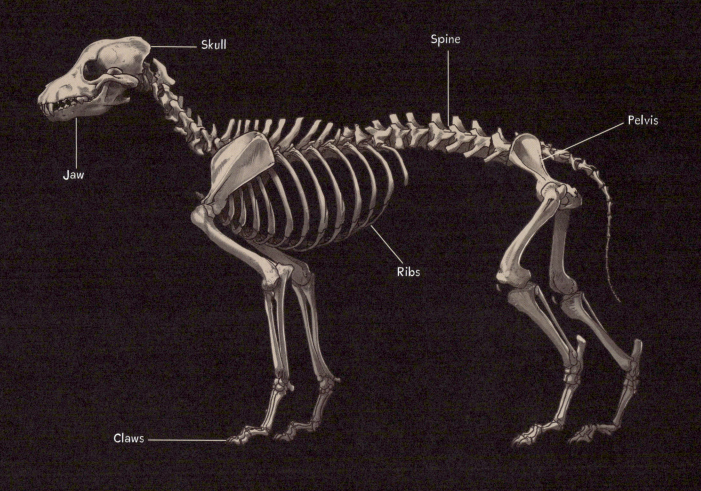

Jaws

Their powerful jaws make it easy to tear apart flesh and bones. They eat every bit of their prey—even the bones!

Teeth

Their 42 very sharp teeth are used to kill and eat their prey.

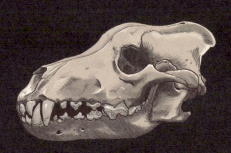

Communication

Arctic wolves howl during hunting, to warn other wolves about prey or danger, when announcing their presence to other wolf packs, and sometimes they howl just for fun! Howls can be heard up to 3 miles (5 kilometres) away.

Packs

There can be as many as 20 Arctic wolves in a pack. Every pack has an alpha male and female, and these are the only ones who have pups. Each pack has a **territory,** an area of land they live in and protect. A wolf can even be killed for entering another pack's territory.

Weight

99 to 154 pounds (45 to 70 kilograms)

Length

3 to 6 feet (91 to 183 centimetres)

Caribou

Caribou are members of the deer family. They are the only deer species where both the males and females have antlers. Barren ground caribou are the most common type of caribou in Canada.

Illustrated by: Amiel Sandland

Range

Barren ground caribou are found throughout Nunavut, in the Northwest Territories, and in northern parts of Manitoba and Saskatchewan at certain times of the year. All types of caribou **migrate**, which means they travel very long distances at different times of the year to find food or give birth.

Babies

Baby caribou are called "calves." They can walk a few hours after they are born. They drink milk from their mothers for the first few weeks, then eat plants.

Caribou mothers are very watchful over their babies to make sure they stay away from danger.

Diet

The caribou's main food source is lichen, a plant that grows mostly on rocks. Barren ground caribou arrive in Nunavut to have their babies just in time for the lichen to bloom, so there is lots to eat. They also eat grassy plants and willow leaves.

Herd

In the winter, male and female caribou live in separate groups, with the calves staying with their mothers. In the spring, the groups join as a single herd to make their long migration. Each herd is led by one caribou that makes sure the herd is safe. The largest herd in Canada is *Qamanirjuaq*, which has hundreds of thousands of members!

Skeleton

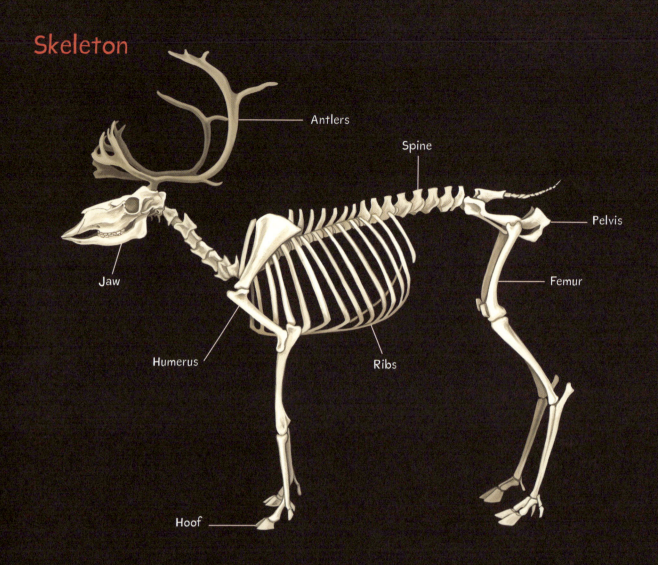

Teeth

Their wide, flat teeth are ground down by their constant chewing, so their teeth are always growing!

Hooves

Their large hooves act as paddles to help them move quickly through the water. Adults can swim 4 to 6 miles (6.5 to 10 kilometres) per hour when they need to.

Antlers

Their antlers fall off once a year, and then regrow, which is called **shedding.** The antlers are covered in a soft, fuzzy material called **velvet.** Male and female caribou use their antlers to defend themselves, and males use them to fight each other for the attention of females.

Weight

Males: 300 pounds (136 kilograms)
Females: 200 pounds (91 kilograms)

Fun Facts

Caribou are very fast! They can run between 37 and 49 miles (60 and 79 kilometres) per hour. That helps them outrun animals that want to hunt them.

Lemming

Lemmings don't hibernate during the winter. They dig tunnels through the snow that reach the **permafrost** (the frozen ground), where they can find plants to eat. These tunnels include areas to rest, to have babies, to store food, and even toilet areas! Lemmings usually live for 1 to 2 years.

Illustrated by: Lenny Lishchenko

Range

Lemmings live in northern regions of the globe, including Canada, Alaska, Norway, Greenland, and Russia.

Babies

Lemmings are able to have babies when they're only a few weeks old. A female can have 3 litters in just one summer! They usually have about 6 babies at once, but the litters can be anywhere between 2 and 12 babies. The babies are born underground in the lemming's burrow.

Diet

Lemmings eat moss, grasses, roots, berries, and other plants. They will dig through the snow to find something to eat. They are able to chew and digest very tough plants. Lemmings spend hours every day finding and eating food, and this activity helps keep them warm.

Skeleton

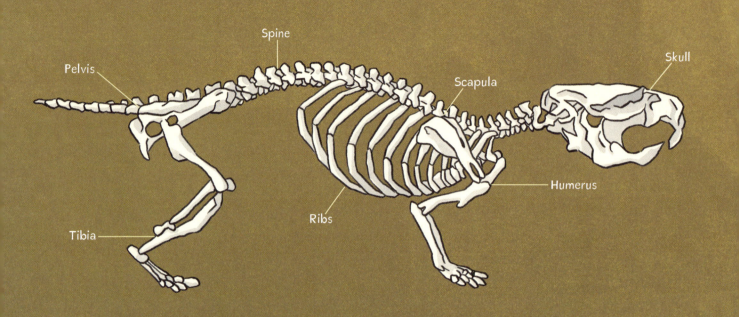

Weight

1 to 3.5 ounces (28 to 99 grams)

Length

2 to 7 inches (5 to 18 centimetres)

Fun Fact

Lemmings' fur is waterproof, and they are able to swim short distances if needed.

Claws

The flat claws on their front feet help them dig in snow and earth.

Teeth

Their sharp teeth never stop growing, and help them chew through tough plants.

Population

Lemming populations go from being very small to very large. This usually happens every 4 years. This can affect the population of other Arctic animals, because so many of them depend on lemmings for food. When lemming populations grow, they migrate in order to find more food.

Muskox

The muskox is a large, hoofed animal. Muskoxen look like bison, but they have long, shaggy hair, a humped back, and very large, curved horns. Males are called "bulls" and females are called "cows." Muskoxen like to live in large groups called "herds." A herd usually has 10 to 25 muskoxen, but can have as many as 60.

Illustrated by: Kagan McLeod

Range

Muskoxen are found on the Arctic tundra. In the summer months, they can be found in valleys, along river banks and lake shores, and in grassy meadows. During the winter, when the wind blows the snow away from hilltops and cliffs, muskoxen move to this higher ground to find food. Muskoxen stay in the Arctic all year long, but they have been known to travel about 60 to 100 miles (97 to 161 kilometres) in search of food.

Babies

A baby muskox is called a "calf." Muskox cows have their calves in March and April. Usually only 1 calf is born, but very rarely a cow has twins. Cows usually move just a short distance away from the herd to have a baby, and will come right back as soon as the baby is able to walk well. Muskox calves can walk well enough to keep up with the herd just a few hours after being born.

Diet

Muskoxen usually eat tundra grasses, Arctic willows, and leaves. During the summer, they can feed anywhere on the tundra where there are lots of grasses and willows growing.

Arctic Willow

Grass

Skeleton

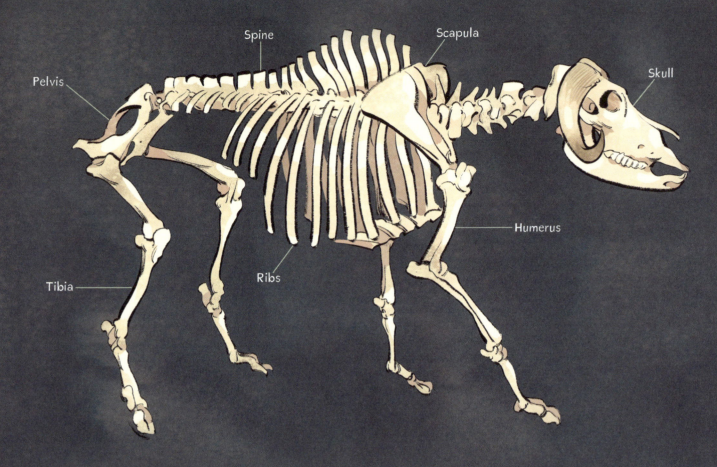

Horns

The horns of the males are much bigger than the females.

Hooves

Their hard hooves can dig up plants from beneath the snow.

Fun Facts

Muskox bulls use their horns to fight each other for the right to be the leader of the herd during mating season. Bulls run toward each other at a full gallop, and the sound their horns make when they hit can be heard from miles away! Bulls will also make loud roaring noises during this time of year to let other bulls know they are ready to fight.

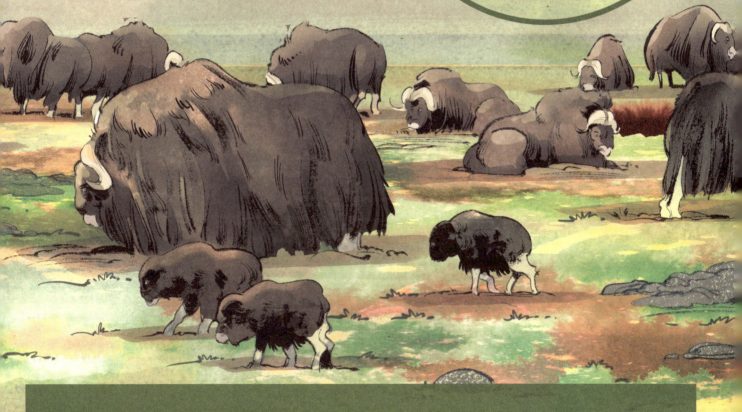

Weight

Males: 595 to 695 pounds (270 to 315 kilograms)

Females: 396 to 496 pounds (180 to 225 kilograms)

Polar Bear

Polar bears' fur appears white for most of their lives, though it yellows as they get older. Their bodies are longer and sleeker than other types of bears. In the wild, polar bears live about 15 to 18 years, but scientists have found some that are over 30 years old! Polar bears are bold, powerful, and surprisingly fast.

Illustrated by: Danny Christopher

Range

Polar bears stay in the Arctic all year round. They travel great distances in search of food. Most bears are land animals, but polar bears live on the land, the sea ice, and in open water. In the summer, they can be found on land and along the shoreline. During the winter they can travel great distances on the sea ice, and they hunt from the ice.

Babies

Baby polar bears are called "cubs." Cubs are born between November and January in dens dug by their mothers. Usually 2 cubs are born, but sometimes 3 are born. The whole time they are in the den, the cubs have only their mother's milk to eat. They leave the den in March or April, as the weather warms up.

Diet

Polar bears are the largest land carnivores in the world. They mainly eat seals, but also eat walruses, muskoxen, caribou, bird eggs, small rodents, and even berries and seaweed. Polar bears will also hunt belugas and narwhals when they become trapped in the sea ice.

Swimming

Polar bears can swim great distances, and they can dive underwater for up to 3 minutes at a time. In the Arctic, polar bears are often seen swimming in deep open water, far away from land. A bear was once tracked swimming more than 400 miles (644 kilometres) on a 9-day journey!

Skeleton

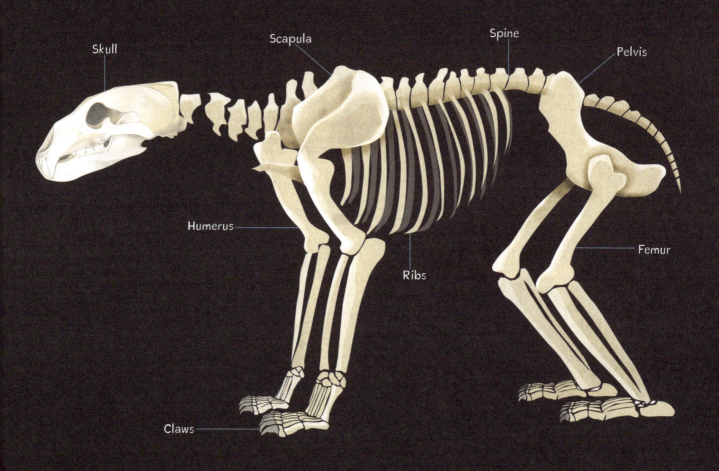

Skull

Their narrow skull helps them cut through water quickly.

Jaws and Teeth

Their powerful jaw contains 42 very sharp teeth.

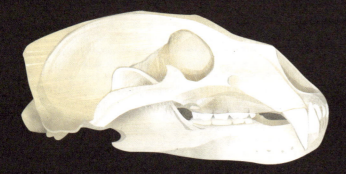

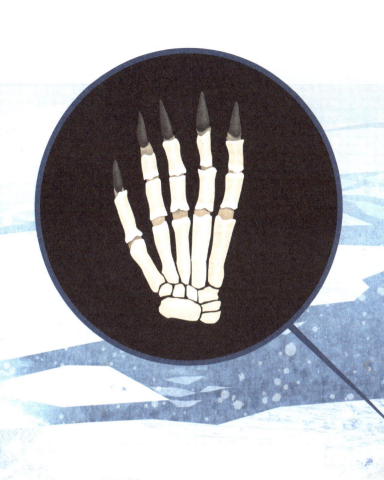

Paws and Claws

Large paws help them walk on snow by spreading their weight over a larger area. When they swim, their paws act like paddles to help them move quickly.

Weight

880 to 1,543 pounds (399 to 700 kilograms). Males can be twice as big as females.

Fun Facts

The biggest polar bear ever caught was found in Kotzebue Sound, Alaska. It stood 11 feet tall (3.4 metres) and weighed 2,200 pounds (998 kilograms)!

Wolverine

The wolverine is the largest member of the weasel family. They are known for their **musk**—a stinky spray they use to keep other animals away! Most wolverines live far from other wolverines, except where there is a good food source. Females stay with their young for about a year while they learn to hunt and survive on their own.

Illustrated by: Patricia Ann Lewis-MacDougall

Range

Wolverines live in most northern areas of the globe. Each wolverine has a **home range**, an area that it uses for hunting that it stays in all year round and protects from other wolverines. Younger males tend to move along with migrating caribou. When young, older, or sick caribou are hunted by predators like wolves or bears, young wolverines scavenge from those hunts.

Babies

A baby wolverine is called a "kit." Female wolverines give birth in the early spring in a den in the snow that is lined with leaves and grass. They make their dens where they are safe from predators, like on cliffs, among heavy willow, or in treed areas. Wolverines usually have 1 to 2 kits, but if food is plentiful, 3 to 5 kits may be born. Kits are born blind and have almost no fur. They are completely white for the first few months of life and then turn black-brown.

Diet

Wolverines are scavengers, and will eat nearly anything they can find! They have also been known to hunt animals much larger than themselves, like muskoxen, moose, and caribou. During the summer months, wolverines usually eat smaller game, such as squirrels, fish, ducks, and young birds, and also eggs and berries. In the wintertime, wolverines eat caribou, muskoxen, moose, deer, seals, foxes, ptarmigans, and rabbits.

Muskox

Ptarmigan

Skeleton

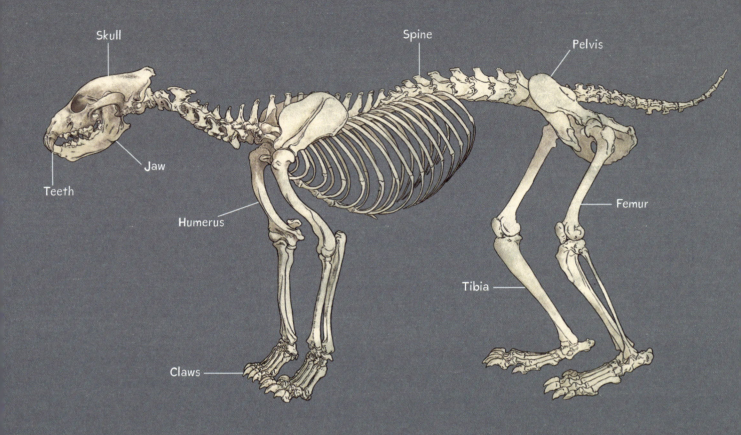

Jaws and Teeth

Their strong jaws and teeth can crunch through bones, and their stomachs can digest the bones, using them for energy and as a source of calcium.

Paws and Claws

Their paws are very strong, with large claws, allowing them to bury food, build dens, and defend themselves from other animals.

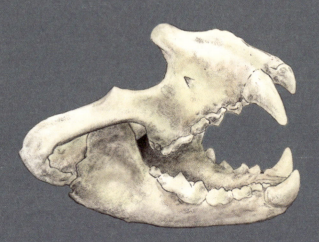

Fun Facts

Wolverines can be found high up in treetops, waiting for danger to pass them by. Wolverines make growling and grunting noises or loudly snap their jaws to communicate. Because of their musk, wolverines are sometimes called "skunk bears"! They can carry pieces of meat much heavier than their own body weight, which they store in their dens for later. They spray their food with their stinky musk so other animals will not find it.

Weight

Males: 30 to 40 pounds (14 to 18 kilograms)
Females: 20 to 25 pounds (9 to 11 kilograms)
A wolverine's weight changes depending on how successful it is at finding food.

AUTHORS

This book includes traditional knowledge and contributions from the following people:

DAVID AGLUKARK (deceased) and DOROTHY AGLUKARK are respected Elders from Arviat, Nunavut.

JAYPEETEE ARNAKAK is a linguist, translator, and educator. He has also adapted several traditional Inuit stories into children's storybooks.

WILLIAM FLAHERTY is a conservation officer and avid hunter who regularly volunteers with Iqaluit Search and Rescue. He lives in Iqaluit, Nunavut.

MONICA ITTUSARDJUAT is from Igloolik, Nunavut. She has worked as a teacher, Inuktitut language coordinator, editor, and translator.

BRIAN KOONOO is from Pond Inlet, Nunavut. He's a resource management officer, and continues to hunt and provide country food for his family, relatives, and community.

ALLEN NIPTANATIAK is a hunter and trapper from Kugluktuk, Nunavut.

GLOSSARY OF INUKTITUT WORDS

The pronunciation guides in this book are intended to support non-Inuktitut speakers in their reading of Inuktitut words. These pronunciations are not exact representations of how the words are pronounced by Inuktitut speakers. For more resources on how to pronounce Inuktitut words, visit inhabitmedia.com/inuitnipingit.

WORD	PRONUNCIATION	DEFINITION
Inuit Qaujimajatuqangit	in-OO-eet KAH-oo-yee-mah-yah-too-KAH-ngeet	Inuit traditional principles
Ulu	OO-loo	crescent knife traditionally used by women
Qamanirjuaq	kah-MAH-nerr-joo-ahk	the name of a caribou herd

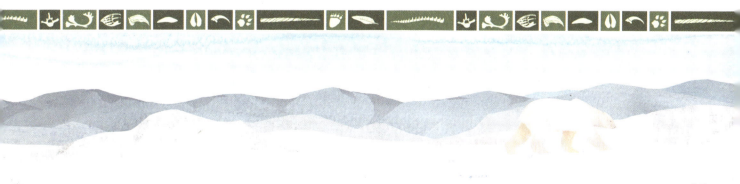

INHABIT
MEDIA
Iqaluit • Toronto